TOP SECRET SCIENCE IN

MEDICINE

Ellen Rodger

CRABTREE

TOP SECRET SCIENCE

Author: Ellen Rodger

Editors: Honor Head, Sarah Eason, Harriet McGregor, and Janine Deschenes

Proofreaders: Sally Scrivener, Tracey Kelly, and Wendy Scavuzzo

Editorial director: Kathy Middleton

Design: Jeni Child

Cover design: Paul Myerscough and Jeni Child

Photo research: Rachel Blount

Production coordinator and prepress technician: Ken Wright

Print coordinator: Katherine Berti

Consultant: David Hawksett

Produced for Crabtree Publishing by Calcium Creative

Photo Credits:

t=Top, tr=Top Right, tl=Top Left

Inside: Flickr: U.S. Army photo by Tom Faulkner: p. 15; RevMedX: p. 12b; Shutterstock: 1000 Words: p. 19; Adriaticfoto: p. 7; Africa Studio: pp. 23, 37; Anyaivanova: p. 24; Blamb: p. 29; Davide Calabresi: pp. 4–5t; Giovanni Cancemi: pp. 22, 45; CLIPAREA l Custom media: pp. 16, 44; Decade3d–anatomy online: p. 34; Adam Jan Figel: p. 39; Juan Gaertner: p. 36; GiroScience: p. 40; Gorodenkoff: pp. 6, 26; Image Point Fr: p. 8; Khuruzero: p. 5r; Kateryna Kon: pp. 11, 33; Lightspring: pp. 3, 41; Master Video: p. 21; MDGRPHCS: p. 32; Orange Deer studio: p. 18; Pop Paul-Catalin: p. 20; Photographee.eu: pp. 28, 42–43; Science photo: pp. 38; SergeBertasiusPhotography: p. 27; Shutterstock: p.1; StockPhotosLV: pp. 12–13t; Succulent: p. 25; TisforThan: p. 35; Vitstudio: p. 42; Jonathan Weiss: p. 31; Whitehoune: p. 14; Yngsa: p. 30; Wikimedia Commons: Karl-Friedrich Höcker: p. 10; Otis Historical Archives Museum of Health and Medicine: p. 9.

Cover: Shutterstock: Science Photo

Library and Archives Canada Cataloguing in Publication

Rodger, Ellen, author
    Top secret science in medicine / Ellen Rodger.

(Top secret science)
Includes index.
Issued in print and electronic formats.
ISBN 978-0-7787-5994-2 (hardcover).--
ISBN 978-0-7787-6032-0 (softcover).--
ISBN 978-1-4271-2243-8 (HTML)

    1. Medicine--Research--Juvenile literature. 2. Drugs--Research--Juvenile literature. 3. Pharmacy--Research--Juvenile literature. I. Title.

R850.R63 2019   j610.72   C2018-905660-6
                                C2018-905661-4

Library of Congress Cataloging-in-Publication Data

Names: Rodger, Ellen, author.
Title: Top secret science in medicine / Ellen Rodger.
Description: New York, New York : Crabtree Publishing, [2019] | Series: Top secret science | Audience: Ages 10-14. | Audience: Grades 7 to 8. | Includes index.
Identifiers: LCCN 2018053376 (print) | LCCN 2018054837 (ebook) | ISBN 9781427122438 (Electronic) | ISBN 9780778759942 (hardcover) | ISBN 9780778760320 (pbk.)
Subjects: LCSH: Medicine--Research--Juvenile literature. | Medicine--History--Juvenile literature. | Medical ethics--Juvenile literature. | Business and medicine--Juvenile literature.
Classification: LCC R130.5 (ebook) | LCC R130.5 .R63 2019 (print) | DDC 610.72--dc23
LC record available at https://lccn.loc.gov/2018053376

Crabtree Publishing Company

www.crabtreebooks.com   1-800-387-7650

Printed in the U.S.A./042019/CG20190215

Published in Canada
Crabtree Publishing
616 Welland Ave.
St. Catharines, ON
L2M 5V6

Published in the United States
Crabtree Publishing
PMB 59051
350 Fifth Avenue, 59th Floor
New York, NY 10118

Published in the United Kingdom
Crabtree Publishing
Maritime House
Basin Road North, Hove
BN41 1WR

Published in Australia
Crabtree Publishing
Unit 3 – 5 Currumbin Court
Capalaba
QLD 4157

CONTENTS

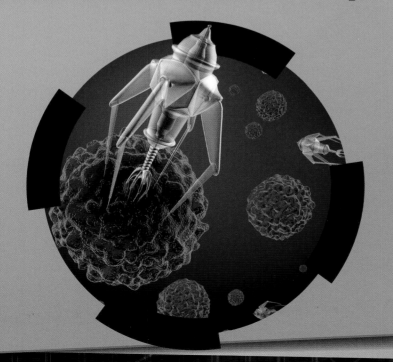

CHAPTER 1

THE CUTTING EDGE

At this moment, medical scientists all over the world are working on cures for diseases that plague our planet. Surgeons are perfecting life-saving surgeries, and researchers are testing breakthrough treatments and **vaccines**. Medical research is expensive and time-consuming work. A new drug could take 20 years from idea to testing and final product. That is why medical secrets are so closely guarded.

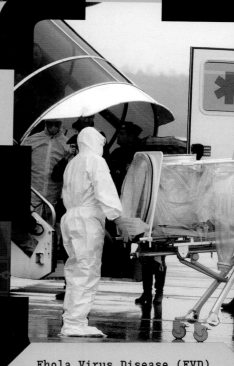

Ebola Virus Disease (EVD) is a disease that spreads through bodily fluids. Here, researchers are testing ways to transport a patient while keeping medical workers safe.

DOLLARS IN POCKETS

Many people and companies are carrying out research to come up with treatments for the same diseases and disorders. Nobody wants their competitors to get ahead of them. **Pharmaceutical**, or drug, companies **invest** in research. This means they spend huge sums of money and years of effort researching, testing, and selling drugs. If the research leads to an effective drug or cure, it becomes in high demand—people and governments will pay a lot of money for it. All of this makes research and development (R&D) in medicine a top secret science. So much is at stake. Pharmaceutical companies will go to great lengths to protect these investments. They keep their laboratories secure and do not accept anyone stealing ideas or drug formulas, or sharing **trade secrets**.

WHEN SECRETS COST DOLLARS

Stealing medical research can cost billions of dollars. In 2011, a researcher was found guilty of stealing secret information from St. Jude Medical, the company that had employed him. The researcher used the stolen information to start a similar company in China and make money from St. Jude's research. The court in California ordered him to pay St. Jude Medical $2.3 billion.

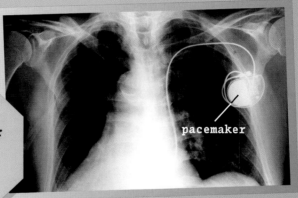

pacemaker

Companies that make medical devices, such as the **pacemaker** shown here on a chest X-ray, guard their research secrets from their competitors.

DARK SCIENCE SECRETS

In 2001, Ellen Roche volunteered for a Johns Hopkins School of Medicine research study on the causes of **asthma**. She inhaled a drug, hexamethonium, meant to cause a mild asthma attack that researchers could study. Instead, Roche became very sick and died a month later. The **U.S. Food & Drug Administration (FDA)** found that the study did not properly protect its volunteers or warn them of the risks. It also found that the researchers did not do enough research to determine that the drug was **toxic** when inhaled. Roche's family **sued** Johns Hopkins and won. Johns Hopkins was made to pay the family a large sum of money.

IMPORTANCE OF RESEARCH

Without experimentation, medical science cannot advance. We would have little knowledge of how the human body works, or how to prevent, treat, and cure diseases. Our knowledge of what does and does not work has grown from research and hundreds of years of trial and error. To come up with new medical treatments and cures, researchers build upon what is already known.

FUDGING RESULTS

A lot of research is made available in medical journals. These **publications** provide scientists and doctors with the latest discoveries. They include long articles about detailed scientific studies. Other experts in the field review the research articles before they are published. But sometimes researchers secretly change their results. Occasionally, they steal ideas from other researchers. Some even make misleading conclusions by sharing only part of the results of their studies. This alters their findings in a way that benefits them. Just a small number of researchers do this, but the impact can be dangerous if the public believe their findings.

A researcher's job can be risky. Some medical research involves working with dangerous diseases. People wear safety gear to keep safe.

DARK SCIENCE SECRETS

In 1998, researcher Andrew Wakefield published a journal article that suggested a link between the measles, mumps, and rubella (MMR) vaccine and **autism**. Autism is a developmental disorder in which people communicate and interact with others differently. The article was published in *The Lancet*, one of the world's most respected medical journals.

Wakefield's research involved 12 children and consisted of stories on the children's medical histories. His research was later proven false and he lost his medical license. Other larger research studies failed to prove any link between the MMR vaccine and autism. *The Lancet* removed the paper, but the damage was done. To this day, many people mention Wakefield's research when refusing to give their children the MMR vaccination. Some reject all vaccines, despite years of proven research on their safety and success. Sadly, this has lead to outbreaks of diseases such as measles and whooping cough in populations where they were previously rare.

THE RISKS OF RESEARCH

Medical research is not without risk. From drug dosages and combinations to complicated surgeries, developing medical treatments relies on trial and error. This means that research studies can have both good and bad results. Over the years, governments and regulatory bodies have developed special rules and methods to follow. These make research safer. Still, errors and accidents happen. Researchers can lose their jobs and damage their reputations following an error, so in rare instances, they keep them secret.

TRIALS AND TRIBULATIONS

Clinical trials are studies performed on people. They are the main way that medical researchers find out if a new drug or surgery works. Research that uses people is tricky—researchers do not want to harm anyone, even though it is always a possibility. That is why rules for medical research include trials that go through different phases. At each phase, more information is gathered from the people participating in the trials.

Despite all precautions, clinical trials still carry some risk to people who participate in them.

KEEPING DRUG SECRETS

Drug companies pay for research trials, or test their own product. This means money is at stake. If things are not going well, drug companies may end trials before they get to the final stage. This means they do not make any money.

Some drug companies have hidden the dangerous side effects of drugs in order to not lose money. But if their secrets are discovered, they could be made to pay huge fines to the government. They might also be sued by people taking the drugs. In 2012, pharmaceutical company GlaxoSmithKline paid a $3 billion fine for withholding the results of studies that showed its **diabetes** drug, Avandia, increased the risk of heart attacks.

DARK SCIENCE SECRETS

Once called a "wonder drug," thalidomide was a mild sleep aid given to pregnant women to help relieve nausea. German company Grünenthal said the drug was safe to use, but trials did not include tests on the effects of the drug used during pregnancy. When women taking the drug began to have babies with **birth defects**, some doctors took note. In 1961, the drug was pulled in West Germany, the United Kingdom, and Australia. Doctors in Canada continued to prescribe it for another year. An estimated 24,000 babies worldwide were born with **malformed**, or badly formed, limbs because of thalidomide. The drug was never used in the United States.

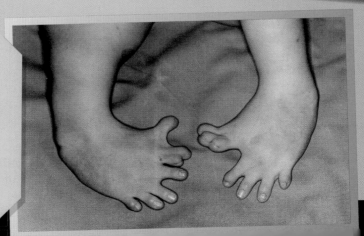

Some survivors of thalidomide in Canada were awarded **compensation**, or money, from the government in 2015, more than 50 years after they were born with deformities caused by the drug.

USING HUMANS FOR RESEARCH

Thousands of years ago, Greek physician Hippocrates of Cos wrote an **oath**, or promise, to help the sick and "do no harm." He pledged that he would not poison people and that whatever he would see or hear would be kept a "holy secret." His words became known as the Hippocratic Oath. It was the first known statement of **medical ethics**, or standards for good behavior.

INFORMED CONSENT

Although most doctors and medical researchers do not swear the Hippocratic Oath today, they do follow guidelines for treatment and research. Under treatment guidelines, patients and research participants are supposed to have full knowledge of any harm a drug or treatment could cause, especially in medical trials. This is called **informed consent**, or the right to know. It is a fairly recent idea. Patients and research participants have to sign forms giving their permission for things such as an operation or drug administration.

Josef Mengele (center) was one of around 30 doctors who experimented on people held as prisoners in concentration camps during World War II (1939-1945). Many of the doctors were put on trial after the war, but Mengele escaped and fled to South America.

BEFORE CONSENT

More than 70 years ago, informed consent was not considered important. Many frightening experiments took place without the knowledge or consent of patients. The most well-known experiments were carried out by doctors working for the **Nazi regime** during World War II. They used people in concentration camps for their research and subjected them to horrifying tests and operations. None of the people consented to the experiments, which were unknown to the outside world. They only came to light after the war, when 23 Nazi doctors were put on trial for **war crimes**.

Some were charged with mass murder. Most of the doctors were found guilty and sentenced to prison or death. The trial was known as the Nuremberg Doctors Trial. It led to the Declaration of Geneva in 1948, in which every doctor in the world was urged to pledge an oath to **humanitarian** goals in medicine.

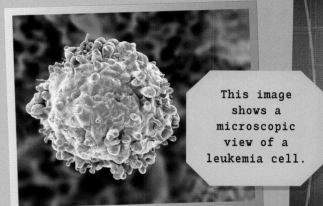

This image shows a microscopic view of a leukemia cell.

TOMORROW'S SECRETS

Pharmaceutical drugs save lives, but drug testing can still be very risky—and even deadly. In 2016, drug company Juno Therapeutics was testing a new drug therapy for leukemia, a type of blood cancer. All participants were patients who had a form of leukemia and all gave informed consent. The trial was halted after five patients died of swelling of the brain. Juno spent months researching the deaths and made the results public. The company is using the research findings to make a safer treatment that is already in early stage trials.

CHAPTER 2

MEDICINE AND WAR

War is brutal, and battlefield injuries are often terrible to body and mind. But war is also a time of great medical inventiveness—some of it top secret and most of it cutting edge. The lessons learned in decades of battlefield medicine have also had great influence on the research and treatment we use in ordinary hospitals today.

Saving lives on the battlefield requires quick action. The faster soldiers receive treatment, the more likely they are to survive.

HEALING WOUNDS

Battlefield medicine has come a long way from **cauterizing** wounds with boiling oil in the 1500s, or tying **tourniquets** made from cotton cloth in the 1900s. Today's wound treatment is high tech and created in labs by companies such as RevMedx, which has developed an injectable sponge in its labs. The sponge expands to fill wounds in areas not protected by body armor. The exact formula for RevMedx's tiny XSTAT sponges is a secret. They can be used to minimize blood loss for up to four hours, giving a wounded soldier time to be transported for surgery.

These tiny RevMedx sponges are inside a syringe. From there, they are injected into wounds.

SAVING LIVES

As an added benefit, RevMedx sponges have tiny objects called markers that give their location when viewed on an X-ray. This means that surgeons can remove them properly when repairing the wound. The sponges first started saving soldiers' lives in 2016. RevMedx hopes they will also be used by paramedics and hospitals for gunshot victims. These cutting-edge wound dressings improve survival rates.

TOMORROW'S SECRETS

In 1862, during the Battle of Shiloh in the U.S. Civil War, more than 16,000 men were wounded. Many lay on the cold, rain-soaked battlefield for days—and their gaping wounds began to glow blue-green. Strangely, in a time before drugs were used to treat infections, the soldiers with glowing wounds had a better survival rate. The glow was a mystery until 2001, when two teenagers toured the battle site and did some research. The work of the teenagers found that the glow came from *Photorhabdus luminescens*, a **bacteria** that lives in the gut of tiny worms called nematodes. The worms had entered the wounds and vomited up the glowing bacteria. *Photorhabdus luminescens* fight off other bacteria and infections. This discovery may lead to amazing new **antibiotics** that could revolutionize medicine in the future.

SUPER-SECRET SUPER-SOLDIERS

Captain America is a comic book and movie series about Steve Rogers, a scrawny man who is rejected by the military in World War II because he is too weak to fight. Rogers is determined to serve his country, so he agrees to take part in a secret military super-soldier project. He is then given a drug that gives him superhuman powers, and becomes Captain America. The story is fictional, but the research being done today to make real-life superhuman soldiers is fact.

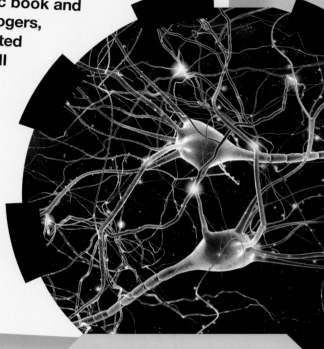

SOLDIERS WHO DEFY DEATH

The Defense Advanced Research Projects Agency (DARPA) is an agency of the U.S. Department of Defense. DARPA develops new technologies. Like many government agencies, its goals may be stated, but its methods are secret. One of DARPA's objectives is to make "kill proof" soldiers. DARPA

The brain is a network of nerves. In a soldier, this network could work like a computer with some medical help (see opposite).

projects aim to produce soldiers with greater endurance, improved senses and strength, and the ability to withstand poisoning from chemicals in enemy attacks.

BRAIN UPLOADS

One current DARPA project is the creation of **software** that can be uploaded directly to the human brain. The software would give soldiers stronger senses, such as improved eyesight and hearing. Currently, DARPA is researching how the brain could "network" like a computer. Its Neural Engineering System Design program is designed to be surgically implanted into a soldier's brain to translate **computer code**, or language.

TOMORROW'S SECRETS

Raytheon seems like a name that comic book superhero Tony Stark (Iron Man) would use for one of his inventions, but it is the name of a technology company based in the United Kingdom. It seems fitting that the company is working with DARPA on a human **exoskeleton**, or external skeleton, that would make every soldier an "Iron Man." The lightweight armor skeleton is robotic, so it will allow soldiers to carry loads far heavier than they would normally be able to. It will also protect soldiers' shoulders, hips, knees, backs, and ankles. The exoskeleton is still in the experimental stage, but researchers think Iron Man soldiers could be deployed during a war sometime in the future.

This soldier is being fitted with an experimental exoskeleton to help improve his mission performance and reduce **fatigue**, or tiredness.

MILITARY GUINEA PIGS

Many countries have used their own soldiers as test subjects for medical experiments—and often without asking the soldiers' consent. Other soldiers consented with little knowledge of the experiments' short- and long-term effects. Soldiers make excellent test subjects because there are usually many in one place, they believe in duty, and they are used to following orders.

TEST SUBJECTS

Experts believe the U.S. military used thousands of soldiers to test the effects of new weapons such as gases and **viruses**, or tiny infectious agents, from 1922 to 1975. These weapons were called chemical weapons and germ warfare. Everything was top secret. Even the soldiers used did not know what was being tested. In 2015, former soldiers suffering from a number of diseases or injuries sued the U.S. army and won. They wanted details of the tests carried out on them. The tests ranged from **mustard gas** exposure during World War II, to **biological warfare** experiments in the 1960s and 1970s. The win meant the U.S army would pay for the veterans' ongoing medical care.

Biological warfare uses viruses like this one, as well as bacteria and toxins, to fight an enemy.

TEST CIVILIANS

Harold Blauer checked into the New York **Psychiatric** Institute for **depression** in 1953, and ended up a test subject in a secret U.S army experiment. Depression is a mood disorder that makes people feel sad, and often hopeless. Blauer did not know that the Institute did testing work for the army, and he became a guinea pig for a drug that produced **hallucinations**. To hallucinate means to see things that do not exist. He died after he was given five injections of the drug. The cause of his death was covered up for more than two decades. In 1987, Blauer's family sued the government and was awarded $700,000 for their loss.

DARK SCIENCE SECRETS

Secret military medical research has fueled discoveries in everything from vaccines for diseases such as yellow fever, to new methods of extracting information from prisoners. Some discoveries were made just by issuing pills to soldiers. That is exactly what the Nazi regime did during World War II. German soldiers were issued packs of Pervitin, also known as methamphetamine. Pervitin kept soldiers awake and energetic for days at a time. It may have contributed to the quick and crushing defeat of France in 1940. But many soldiers became addicted, a few died of heart attacks, and some became **psychotic**.

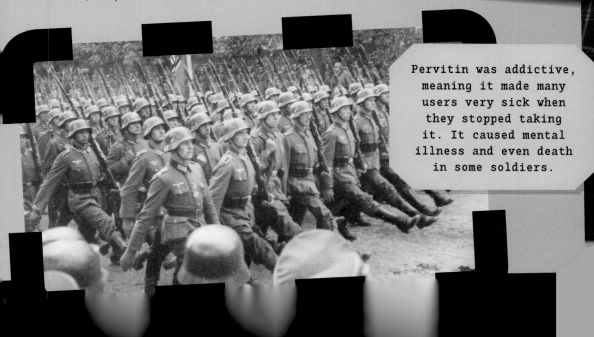

Pervitin was addictive, meaning it made many users very sick when they stopped taking it. It caused mental illness and even death in some soldiers.

CHEMICAL SECRETS

Phosgene, mustard gas, chlorine gas, napalm, sarin—they are all grisly chemicals that were used or developed during war. Chemistry has provided researchers with any number of toxic and terrible weapons. And they have all been tested on humans—some secretly and some openly. Chemical and biological weapons are not "allowed" during war. International law **prohibits**, or forbids, the production, **stockpiling**, and use of these deadly agents. But they were secretly used.

SARIN EXPERIMENTS

Twenty-year-old soldier Ronald Maddison just wanted a three-day **pass**, or time off, and some cash when he volunteered for a British army experiment in 1953. He would never get the chance to use that pass. At a science and technology laboratory, army medical scientists dosed Maddison with 0.007 ounces (200 mg) of sarin. Within 30 minutes, he began thrashing and foaming at the mouth. He then became unconscious and could not be **revived**, or woken up. Maddison's death was covered up for 51 years.

Sarin is a colorless, odorless liquid. It is made up of hydrogen, carbon, oxygen, fluorine, and phosphorus. It is quite deadly.

$C_4H_{10}FO_2P$

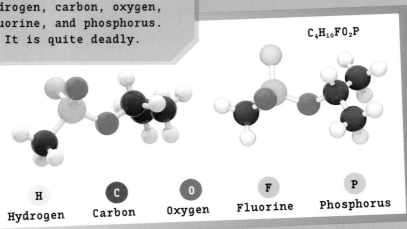

H	C	O	F	P
Hydrogen	Carbon	Oxygen	Fluorine	Phosphorus

FINDING ANSWERS

A secret investigation into Maddison's death was held in 1953, and a public investigation in 2004. His father was the only member of his family allowed to attend the first one. He was warned to never share any information. The full report on Maddison's death was not released and no one apologized for his death. At the second inquest, in 2004, Maddison's family was finally given the gruesome details of his unlawful death. Later, it was revealed that thousands of other British soldiers suffered the effects of decades of secret drug tests conducted through the 1980s.

This army officer is wearing protective clothing to search for evidence related to the poisoning of the Skripals.

DARK SCIENCE SECRETS

The nerve agent, or poison, Novichok was secretly created by military scientists from the **Soviet Union** in the 1970s and 1980s. When the Soviet Union broke up, Russia took over the research. Rumors say it was used on people the Russian government wanted to kill. In 2018, former Russian spy Sergei Skripal and his daughter Yulia were poisoned with Novichok. The two were found unconscious on a public bench in Salisbury, England, where they lived. They spent weeks recovering in hospital while doctors treated them. The British government believes Russia is responsible for secretly poisoning the Skripals.

CHAPTER 3

EXPERIMENTATION

Surgery is one of the oldest medical fields. It is used to repair damage or get rid of disease by cutting into the body. This medical specialty is practiced by doctors with special training. They learn as much "on the job" by operating on bodies—dead and alive—as through textbooks and lectures. This means surgery can be experimental—doctors can find out what works and does not by working on bodies. Because of this, new or previously untried surgeries may also be secretive.

Augmented reality headsets allow surgeons to see vital information about the patient while performing surgery, without looking away from the procedure.

CUTTING-EDGE SURGERY

Surgery is now so common that people hardly bat an eye at the word. Most people will have a surgery at some point in their life. Depending on the job, that surgery could be done by a human surgeon in an operating theater or by a guided robot acting on a surgeon's instructions. In the very near future, surgery might use **virtual reality (VR)** to extend a human surgeon's abilities. Surgeons are already experimenting with augmented reality headsets to help them carry out complex surgery. These headsets are worn by the surgeon, and mix the real world with the computer-generated world.

TRICKY TRANSPLANTS

Head **transplants** are currently found only in the movies. In reality, doctors have never successfully attached a head from one person to the body of another. They have secretly experimented by attaching animal heads to animal bodies, however.

The first **partial** face transplant took place in 2005, when a woman who had been attacked by a dog received a new nose and mouth. By 2015, the procedure had improved. A fireman injured in a fire received a full face transplant. His new face was that of a 26-year-old who died in a biking accident.

This surgeon is guiding a robot called Da Vinci during a surgical procedure.

TOMORROW'S SECRETS

Each year, 468,000 people in the United States are placed on **dialysis** due to kidney disease and failure. Dialysis is a process that removes waste from a patient's blood, a job that the kidney usually does. Dialysis keeps the patient alive, but it is only a temporary solution. Currently, the only permanent solution is a kidney transplant from a **donor**, or a person who agrees to give a body part or parts to a sick person. But this is rare. However, researchers at the University of California in San Francisco (UCSF) will soon carry out human trials on an **artificial**, or human-made, kidney. UCSF's Kidney Project uses living cells and other technologies inside the artificial kidney, which looks like a small gray box, to make it function like the real organ.

MAKING ORGANS

Fifty years ago, the world's first heart transplant took place. Then and now, the only way to **legally**, or lawfully, get a new heart was to take a healthy one donated by a person who is **clinically dead**. Now scientists are working on creating new hearts and other organs from **stem cells**, and using new technology to make artificial organs.

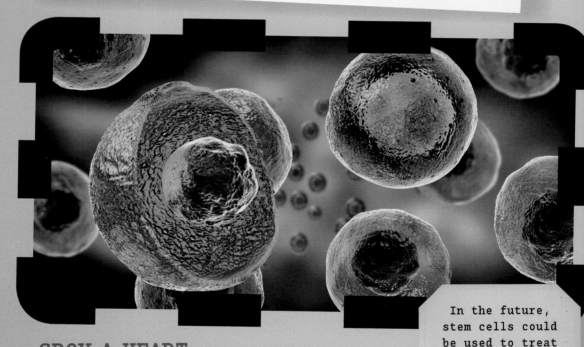

GROW A HEART

Scientists at Columbia University grew the first functioning human heart muscle in 2018. Using stem cells, the scientists were able to grow the muscle in a lab in four weeks. The researchers made the muscle twitch and beat with electrical pulses. Their goal is to grow hearts for research and testing, as well as one day for heart transplants.

In the future, stem cells could be used to treat many diseases and injuries, including severe back injuries.

TESTS AND TRIALS

Growing organs such as hearts, livers, and kidneys from stem cells in a lab is called **tissue engineering**. Most tissue engineering projects are in the lab research stage, which makes the details on how it is done a secret. When they advance to clinical trials, researchers will be required to make sure human test subjects know what they are getting into. Some volunteers would be people whose organs are failing, so they might be desperate for a solution—so desperate that they would gamble their lives on an unproven organ and surgery.

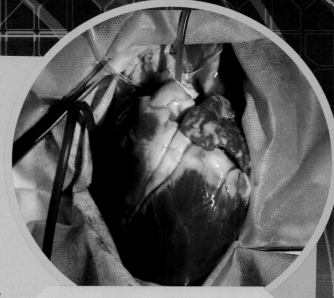

Organs need blood and oxygen to flow through them up until the time they are removed. That is why donors must still be alive when the organs are taken from them.

DARK SCIENCE SECRETS

Organ trading is as chilling as it sounds. It involves people selling parts of themselves for cash. The organ traders buy these parts, and then sell them to sick people who need them. This buying and selling takes place in the **black market**. Black market means the illegal **trade**, or buying and selling, of things. An even scarier part of the black market is the "red market." This is the trade in organs stolen from people. These organs are taken by force, usually from people who have been kidnapped. The **World Health Organization (WHO)** estimates that more than 11,000 organs are sold on the black and red markets every year.

LAB RATS AND HUMAN GUINEA PIGS

Medical studies have many volunteers. People sometimes volunteer because they believe in helping others and advancing science. Others do it because they are already sick and have gone through other treatments without success. Still others are swayed by the cash, if the study is paying people to take part.

HUMAN TESTERS

Human challenge studies are research studies in which a virus is intentionally tested on humans. They have been done for hundreds of years, and they are often done after researchers test a disease and potential treatment on animals in a lab. They are used as the last stage testing of new vaccines. Being deliberately infected with a disease as part of a study sounds like a terrible idea. But every year, hundreds of people do it to advance medical science.

Mice and rats are usually the first live test subjects for new treatments. Human studies come later.

ANIMAL TESTERS

Most drugs and vaccines are tested on animals before they are tested on humans. Without animal test subjects, we would not have many lifesaving drugs or vaccines for diseases such as polio, smallpox, and even rabies. But animal research is very secretive. This is partly because humans do not want to know about or see animals being hurt by medical trials and tests. Also, animals cannot consent. Raising animals for testing is big business. People make money from testing animals. Most countries have laws on animal testing, but animal protection groups say there are safe ways to test many new medical innovations without using animals.

These animal rights activists in Oregon are protesting outside a medical research facility against the use of animals in medical tests and experiments.

TOMORROW'S SECRETS

Diabetes is a disease in which a person's pancreas cannot produce **insulin**, a substance that helps control sugar in the blood. It affects 415 million people all over the world and an estimated 3.4 million die of diabetes-related health issues each year. Right now there is no cure, but diabetes can be treated. Researchers developed a safe treatment for diabetes in 1922, testing it first on dogs and rabbits. That treatment—insulin made from other sources—is still used daily by millions of people.

Current research is on developing drug treatments that last longer, and on finding a cure. One experiment involves using stem cells. Researchers grew healthy mice pancreas cells in rat **embryos**. The cells were then transplanted into diabetic mice. The cells reversed the diabetes. The next step will be testing this in humans.

EXPERIMENTING WITH DRUGS

Testing drugs happens in labs and hospitals all around the world. Many countries have laws that regulate testing, but many do not, or the rules they have are weak. Even with good laws, some researchers do not follow through.

EXPLOITING PEOPLE?

Much research is carried out by researchers at universities, or by companies that have been paid by pharmaceutical corporations to conduct trials. Some medical research takes advantage of groups of people who enter into testing trials for money or for a potential cure. The test subjects may get a small fee for being a part of a study. It is up to the researchers to inform the subjects about the risks and get their written consent for the tests. Risks could range from temporary soreness to lifelong pain, or even death. If a person is desperate for the money, the fee could seem more important than the risks.

Researchers must keep thorough records of all the studies they carry out.

RISK OF HARM

There is a risk of harm with all studies done on humans. In some cases, researchers do not know if their tests will cause harm. They can only base their ideas on previous tests or knowledge of how the drug works. A 2006 study of a leukemia drug conducted in the United Kingdom left six men in pain in hospital, fighting for their lives. They survived but have been told they may develop cancer or other diseases in the future. The trial of the drug was called the elephant man trial after some test subjects' heads swelled. An investigation of the trial led to new rules in Europe for how drugs are tested on humans. These included not testing all subjects at the same time and ensuring high-risk trials take place in hospitals where people could be quickly helped if things go wrong.

Some homeless and poor people sign up for drug trials because they need the money—no matter what the risk.

DARK SCIENCE SECRETS

According to **bioethicist** Dr. Carl Elliot, more homeless people are now taking part in drug trials because it is easier to convince them to ignore risks. In his research, he found that in the United States, private drug trial companies put advertisements in papers and visit homeless shelters to attract volunteers. Many homeless people volunteer for several trials to earn money. Most of the studies are for psychiatric drugs for mental illnesses, but homeless participants need to stop taking their regular medicine in order to test the drugs. This, and the side effects of taking part in multiple trials, has left them less healthy.

CHAPTER 4

BRAIN WORK

Research into the brain and **nervous system** are fast expanding areas of medical research. Each year, scientists get a better understanding of how the brain works. Billions of dollars are being spent on developing surgeries, drugs, and techniques for exploring the brain and targeting brain diseases and disorders.

About 5.7 million Americans have a brain disease called Alzheimer's. Sufferers experience severe memory loss.

BRAIN MAP

The brain is the body's processing unit. It governs all actions and commands in the body. That explains why it has taken so long to map the brain. Up until 2016, researchers had only partial views of how the brain operates. Then, researchers at a number of universities worked together to map the brain's structure and how this amazing organ works.

The Human Connectome Project was funded by the U.S. government. It mapped the human brain and measured brain function, how cells are organized, and how the brain sends signals. Even with this, researchers say brain exploration is still in the beginning stages. Now that there is a map (or several), brain scientists can use them to forge new paths in disease and disorder research.

UNDERSTANDING BRAIN DISORDERS

Brain disorders are diseases of the body's nervous system. They include mental disorders such as depression. But brain disorders are broad and also include diseases such as **dementia**, a decline in memory and mental ability, and **Parkinson's**, a disease in which brain cells die and affect a person's behavior and movement.

Brain disorder researchers examine all aspects of the brain to understand how it works. Most research builds on the results of earlier studies. That is why research is shared in medical journals.

TOMORROW'S SECRETS

Huntington's disease is a brain disorder in which the brain's cells die, slowly destroying a person's ability to move, talk, and think clearly. Right now, there is no cure for the disease. However, researchers are working on treatments that slow, reverse, and prevent it. In 1994, researchers discovered the disease was **inherited**. In 2015, the first ever drug that targeted the cause of Huntington's was tested in human trials in the United Kingdom, Germany, and Canada. It was successful in reducing a substance in the nervous system that caused the disease—giving hope to people who have the disease, and their children. Further tests must be done before the drug can be released for use.

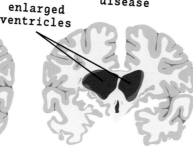

normal brain

ventricles

enlarged ventricles

Huntington's disease

damage to brain tissue

Ventricles are fluid-filled spaces in the brain. They are larger in people with Huntington's disease.

DRUGS AND THE MIND

Many drugs used to treat mental health disorders were discovered by accident or by trial and error. That is what happened when researchers created a new group of drugs for depression and anxiety, called SSRIs. These drugs were medical game changers in the 1980s and 1990s.

HAPPY ACCIDENT

Before the late 1940s, drugs used to treat symptoms of many mental health disorders were limited. Researchers often did not even know which chemicals in the brain were being affected by certain drugs. In the 1950s, doctors in Switzerland discovered the first antidepressants when testing a drug for **schizophrenia**, a disease that affects how a person feels, thinks, and acts. The drug was not good for people with schizophrenia, but they found that it altered chemicals in the brain that controlled moods. It was suited for people with depression and anxiety. Within a few decades, drug companies were using this research to create SSRIs. This new class of drugs increase the levels of a brain chemical called serotonin. It is responsible for mood, sleep, and memory.

People with schizophrenia often suffer **hallucinations**, which are sounds, feelings, or visions that are not real.

DRUG COMPETITION

By 2014, 30 million people in the United States were taking SSRIs. Prozac was the first SSRI antidepressant drug produced in 1987 by Eli Lilly and Co. Lilly had the **patent** for the drug. A patent gives a company the right to prevent other companies from selling a drug with the same makeup. In 2001, the patent ran out. Other companies then produced cheaper versions of the drug.

The SSRI Prozac earned billions of dollars for the drug company Eli Lilly.

DARK SCIENCE SECRETS

For 22 years, from 1953 to 1975, medical researchers working for the U.S. Central Intelligence Agency (CIA) conducted secret drug experiments on soldiers, prison inmates, and civilians in the United States and Canada. Thousands of people took part in several experiments in a project called MKUltra. Some of the participants were given mind-altering drugs such as LSD. The CIA wanted to test whether LSD could be used as a weapon to control people's minds. After taking the LSD, people hallucinated.

A newspaper story in the mid-1970s reported that these experiments were happening. Most of the participants had no idea they were part of CIA experiments. For years, many suffered side effects such as extreme fear. The project was canceled in 1975 and files were destroyed. The U.S. government later outlawed experimenting on humans without their consent. Some victims received compensation for their suffering from their governments.

PAIN IN THE HEAD

Migraines are intense headaches that can include full-body symptoms such as blurred vision and vomiting. They are the third-most common disease in the world. They are also one of the oldest-known ailments, having been mentioned in Hippocrates's writings from 400 B.C.E.

NOT JUST A HEADACHE

For centuries, migraines were thought to be caused by everything from "hot vapors from the stomach" to ill winds. More recent research on the cause of migraines has led to a new drug for this disabling disease.

In 1980, scientists found that a molecule used by **neurons** in the brain was connected to migraines. This molecule is called calcitonin gene-related peptide (CGRP). In 2010, scientists in Montréal, Canada, and Oxford, England, found that the most common form of migraine was caused by a **mutation**, or change, in a gene that affects neuron communication in the brain.

Migraine attacks can last for up to 72 hours. Some people have many attacks each week.

FIRST MIGRAINE PREVENTER

Finding a cause for migraines has helped create new treatments. Once CGRP was identified, work began on ways to keep it from being activated. A new migraine medication that targeted CGRP was developed and released in 2018. It makes migraines less frequent. It is given through a needle. Unlike other migraine medications, it only has to be used once every six months.

This illustration shows neurons in the brain of a person with Parkinson's disease. The red spheres represent substances that build up and damage the neurons.

TOMORROW'S SECRETS

Parkinson's disease is known as a **neurodegenerative disease**. This means that it gradually causes neurons in the brain to stop working correctly. This leads to difficulty walking and talking. There is no cure right now, but brain surgery is improving the way neuron signals communicate. Deep brain stimulation (DBS) involves implanting a device in the brain to send signals. It is not known exactly how deep brain stimulation works, but researchers do know that it helps diminish **tremors**, or shaking, for people with Parkinson's. Research on DBS is also being applied to other brain disorders, such as depression.

CHAPTER 5

PUSHING THE BOUNDARIES

Some researchers study a disease in a lab. Others develop new treatments in surgeries, or by testing animal or human subjects in a trial. Occasionally, researchers do not want to wait for approval to test on others—so they experiment on themselves.

DR. TEST SUBJECT

Medical researchers have been experimenting on themselves for centuries. They may infect themselves with a disease to determine its cause, or take an unproven drug or vaccine to test a cure. In the past, if they died from the test, the medical self-experimentation was often covered up. If they were successful, the daring stunts were written up as feats of bravery.

BACTERIA SOUP

In the early 1980s, Dr. Barry Marshall, an Australian physician, deliberately drank a broth teeming with a type of bacteria that causes stomach ulcers. Dr. Marshall wanted to test his idea that antibiotic drugs could kill the bacteria, *Helicobacter pylori*. After drinking

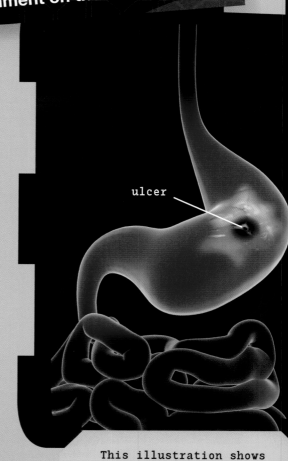

ulcer

This illustration shows an ulcer in the stomach.

the broth, he developed **gastritis**, a disorder that comes before an ulcer. Before his experiment, it was believed that ulcers were caused by stress or too much stomach acid. Marshall thought they were caused by *Helicobacter pylori*, which could be treated and cured with antibiotics. He treated and cured his own gastritis infection with antibiotics. He knew his research would need to be published in a medical journal for his findings to be accepted by other doctors.

He submitted a paper to a journal, but it was rejected. Other medical scientists did not believe ulcers could be cured so easily because they did not fully understand what caused ulcers. It took another 10 years of research and curing people with antibiotics for the medical community to accept Dr. Marshall's findings. In 2005, he won a **Nobel Prize** for his research.

TOMORROW'S SECRETS

Could a worm hold the key to a cure for the breathing disease asthma? That was the question a team of researchers from the University of Nottingham, England, asked in 2004. To begin answering it, Dr. David Pritchard let 50 hookworm larvae burrow into his skin to find out if it was safe to do so. He had observed that people infected with hookworm did not suffer from certain diseases such as hay fever and asthma. He believed the worms somehow led to the patients having fewer **allergic reactions** that trigger asthma attacks. Dr. Pritchard's research is ongoing. His ultimate goal is to reduce allergic reactions without the use of the worms themselves.

Hookworms live off of other living things. These hookworm **larvae**, or young, are inside a human foot.

14:30 PM

SUPER STEM CELLS

If cells are the building blocks of the body and where life begins, stem cells are the body's turbo-charged superhero cells. Stem cells can divide, renew, and turn into other types of body tissue. Modern medical science has now found ways to make them repair and regrow damaged body parts.

Many stem cell treatments are experimental. They have not yet been proven safe or effective.

STEM CELLS TO THE RESCUE!

Since 1961, when the first paper explaining how stem cells could divide and self-renew was published, the pace of stem cell discoveries has increased at lightning speed. Researchers believe they will one day create laboratory cells that can replace any cell in our bodies. Right now, stem cells are used successfully to grow **skin grafts**, and to treat blood cancers such as leukemia, and diseases of the eye.

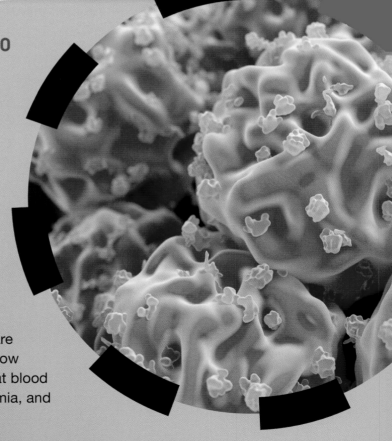

NOSE IN HER BACK

Some experimental stem cell research is carried out on human volunteers. A woman from the United States had stem cells taken from her nose and implanted in her spine at a hospital in Portugal. The cells were supposed to repair nerve damage to her spine and allow her to walk again. Instead, she was later forced to have a 1.2-inch (3-cm), nose-like growth removed from her spine. The story came to light when the results of her surgery were published in the *Journal of Neurosurgery: Spine* in 2014.

TOMORROW'S SECRETS

Researchers at the University of California, Los Angeles (UCLA) may have discovered the cure for baldness. Baldness is not a disease, but in some people, hair loss is a side effect of disease. About 80 million men and women in the United States are fully or partially bald. In 2017, scientists found that hair **follicles** can be grown from skin cells in a lab. They grew hair on shaved mice by transplanting cells into the mice. The research will be used to develop hair regrowth treatments in the future, as well as test drugs that assist hair growth.

Growing hair from transplanted cells may make baldness a thing of the past.

FIGHTING MODERN PLAGUES

When a disease kills 50 percent or more of the people it infects, finding an effective treatment, cure, or vaccine is a top priority. Some modern plagues such as EVD strike suddenly and violently. The work done to control these diseases and develop cures is just as fast paced.

EVD VACCINE

EVD is the leading cause of natural death in chimpanzees and gorillas in the wild. It is also extremely deadly to humans, killing roughly 50 percent of the people it infects. It is thought that humans get it from killing and eating wild animals such as chimps and antelopes. Infected humans pass it on to other people through their blood or other bodily fluids, or even through contact with infected clothing or bedding. In 2015, a human trial for a vaccine used in Guinea, Africa, helped end an EVD outbreak. Researchers had been working on a way to stop the disease since 1976, but vaccine research amped up after the 2014–2016 outbreak left 11,310 people dead. Research is continuing, as EVD has several different **strains**, or types.

Researchers who work on treatments for highly contagious diseases such as EVD must wear protective suits.

AIDS VACCINE

Researchers are working on creating a vaccine for all strains of human immunodeficiency virus (HIV), the virus that causes acquired immunodeficiency syndrome (AIDS). A new vaccine was tested in 2018. The test was to see whether the vaccine was safe to use. Serious adverse reactions were found in only 1 percent of the test subjects. Research and testing on HIV vaccines began in 1984. With each new trial, more is learned about the disease, which has killed 35 million people over the past 35 years. Research is ongoing to create a safe and effective vaccine.

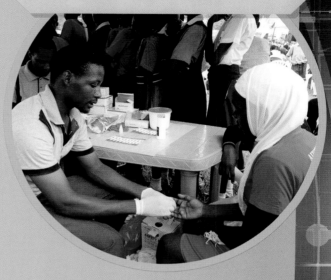

This woman in Uganda is being tested for HIV. About 34 million people are HIV positive, and 69 percent of them live in Africa. Several experimental HIV vaccines are being tested there.

DARK SCIENCE SECRETS

Hundreds of U.S. **foster children** were guinea pigs for an HIV and AIDS drug testing program in the 1980s and 1990s. The tests were conducted by National Institutes of Health (NIH) researchers. The children had HIV, and in the 1980s and 1990s, there were few drug options for prolonging or improving their lives. NIH researchers knew their studies were the only way some of the children could receive drugs for their disease, so many ignored protocols. The mostly poor and minority children suffered normal drug test side effects such as vomiting, rashes, and drops in their ability to fight infections.

In 2005, the Associated Press reported on the drug tests and the government investigated. The NIH was found to have violated research rules. Since the NIH study, some states have changed the way they approve research on foster children.

CHAPTER 6

WHAT NEXT?

Imagine a technology or medicine, impossible to see with the naked eye, that helps improve how drugs work in the human (or other animal) body. Nanomedicine is an emerging field of medical research that promises to change the way diseases are diagnosed and treated.

Nanoparticles are so small that they can pass into a body cell, through its outer layer.

TEENY, TINY TECHNOLOGY

Nanotechnology is an area of science that deals with extremely tiny things about 100 nanometers (nm) (0.0001 mm) in size. To get a rough idea of that size, a sheet of paper in this book is about 100,000 nm (0.1 mm) thick. So, a nanoparticle is a microscopic portion of matter, or substance. In fact, until about 30 years ago, things as small as a nanometer could not even be seen with the strongest microscopes. Scientists now use atomic force microscopes (AFM) to see things on the nanoscale.

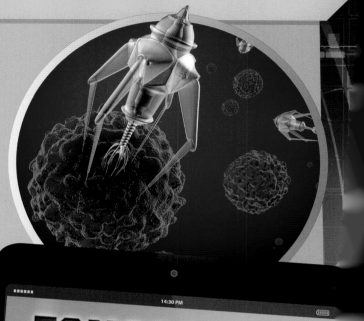

This illustration shows a nano-robot, or nanobot, delivering medicine to a cell. In the future, researchers are hoping nanobots will fight cancer and other diseases in this way.

NANO-ATTACK

Nanomedicine is used in diagnosing illness, and to deliver **chemotherapy** drug treatments to cancer patients. Chemotherapy is a common treatment for many cancers. Chemotherapy drugs kill cancer cells, but they also kill other healthy cells such as hair and digestive cells. Nanoparticles can deliver smaller doses of the drugs directly to the cancer cells, so healthy cells are not also killed. They are "engineered" to swim through barriers and directly reach cancer cells.

Nanoparticles can also be programmed to "time release" drugs so that they are delivered more effectively. A lot of nanomedical research is ongoing and in the testing stages, but researchers already know that nanomedicine can help with respiratory diseases, stomach or gastrointestinal diseases, eye diseases, and brain and nervous system diseases.

TOMORROW'S SECRETS

14:30 PM

Researchers are working on nanoparticle eye drops that deliver drugs for eye diseases. These drops, called nanoemulsions could deliver a new molecule that slows **macular degeneration**. Macular degeneration is the leading cause of vision loss in people over 60 years old. It happens when the **macula**, or the eye's light sensor, wears down. The eye drops may also help with another eye disorder, **retinitis pigmentosa**. It is an inherited eye disorder that causes blindness. So far, researchers have tested the nanoemulsion drops on mice and found that they preserved their sight. The next step is testing on humans.

GENE GENIUS

Sixty years ago, little was known about diseases that are inherited. In some cases, it was not even known that certain diseases were inherited. A massive international research project changed that. It altered the way medical researchers looked for cures for life-threatening diseases such as cancers, cystic fibrosis (CF), and diabetes.

HUMAN GENOME PROJECT

The Human Genome Project (HGP) involved hundreds of researchers investigating all of the **genes** of human beings. Everyone has thousands of genes in the cells of their bodies. Genes carry the information that determines traits such as brown eyes or blonde hair, or in some cases, the likelihood of getting certain diseases. A person's full set of genes is called their genome. The HGP began in 1990, and it took scientists 15 years to map and figure out the order of the genome. In the end, they were able to make links from certain genes to inherited diseases. Because of their research, each year, better tests, drugs, and treatments are developed for many diseases.

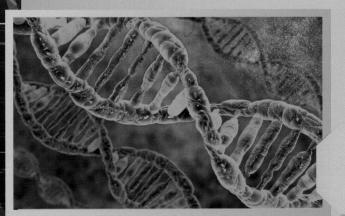

This is an illustration of deoxyribonucleic acid (DNA). DNA carries our genes and is found inside each body cell.

GENE THERAPY

CF is a genetic disease that causes the body to produce thick **mucus** that clogs the lungs. Though the CF gene was discovered in 1989, there is no cure yet. However, with the help of HGP knowledge, researchers have been working on a cure using **gene therapy**.

Gene therapy is a technique that prevents or treats diseases by "fixing" faulty genes or replacing them with new ones. Gene therapy is new and can be risky. In one trial, researchers tried to introduce a virus like a cold to deliver a new, working gene into the body of a person with CF. It failed. In another trial, researchers tried to introduce the new gene in a fat bubble delivered to the lungs. That improved how the lungs worked, but only by a small margin. Researchers are "tweaking" the therapy so that it vastly improves how the lungs work.

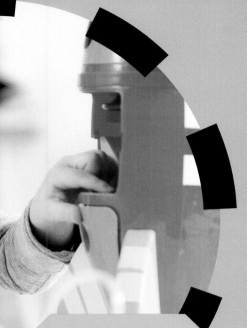

One out of every 3,000 children has CF. Many use a device called a nebulizer (shown here) to breathe in their medication.

DARK SCIENCE SECRETS

Genetic testing kits allow people to swab the inside of their cheeks and send the swab away. Some kits test for ancestry, or where people came from. Others test for the likelihood they will get certain diseases. They all test DNA, which is the hereditary material in all living things. Testing kits have a downside, however, including the fact that a person's genetic information could be sold. Many kit companies have deals with drug firms that use a person's information—without paying him or her—for new drug ideas.

BE A MEDICAL SCIENTIST

Medical research is demanding. No matter how much planning is done, sometimes things go wrong. Medical scientists are highly skilled and must make sure the studies they design are **ethical**, or morally right. Medical science done right can change the world. Think about it. What if you were a medical scientist who found a cure for a new and deadly disease? How great would that be? And how much work would it require?

YOUR MISSION

- Do some research on the history of existing diseases such as EVD or AIDS to see how researchers pieced together the timeline of these diseases. How did they find out where the diseases started? When did they begin? How far did they spread and how quickly?

- Write a research plan on how you will study an entirely new disease. Will you study it in a lab? Or will you travel to where the disease is currently active to observe it?

- How will you deal with the private information that patients give you? What if they told you a secret that was important to the study but they did not want anyone to know? Would you share it with other researchers? Could you find a way of sharing the information without breaking their trust?

Medical research on stem cells from embryos has caused controversy. Some people think that it is not ethical. They believe that destroying an embryo is equal to taking a life.

TOP SECRET

Finding a good treatment or cure for a new disease is important. If you were on the verge of a cure, how would you share what you have learned with other researchers so that they can work on a cure, too?

GLOSSARY

Please note: Some **bold-faced** words are defined where they appear in the book.

allergic reactions When the body reacts abnormally to a substance

antibiotics Drugs that fight infections caused by bacteria

asthma A disease of the lungs that makes it hard for someone to breathe

bacteria Tiny living organisms, some of which cause diseases

bioethicist Someone who studies the morals or values of medical treatments, testing, and procedures

biological warfare Using toxins or viruses as weapons to harm or kill people

birth defects Conditions that people are born with, such as limbs that do not function normally

cauterizing Burning the skin to stop bleeding or prevent infection

clinically dead When the heart stops beating and blood no longer circulates

diabetes A disorder in which the body does not produce insulin or cannot use it properly

embryos A very early stage in the development of babies

follicles The sacs from which hairs grow

foster children Children who live with a family that is not their birth family while they wait to be adopted

humanitarian Concerned about other humans, acts to help others

inherited Something, such as a disorder or disease, that a person gets genetically from a direct relative

invest To put money into something

mucus A slippery bodily substance

mustard gas A chemical that causes burning of the eyes and lungs

Nazi regime The ruling government of Germany from 1933 to 1945

nervous system The brain, spinal cord, and all the connecting neurons that transmit information around the body

neurons Nerve cells in the central nervous system that receive, process, and transmit information through the brain and body

Nobel Prize An international award given for exceptional accomplishments in several fields such as medicine, chemistry, and peace

pacemaker Device that keeps the heart beating regularly

partial Part of something

psychiatric Related to the study and treatment of mental disorders

psychotic Unable to determine what is reality

publications Reproductions of something such as a magazine or journal, made available for a larger audience

skin grafts A transplant of skin from one area of the body to another, or from one person to another

software Computer operating program

Soviet Union A union of 15 countries in eastern Europe and Asia from 1922 to 1991

stem cells Cells in a body that can grow into many different cell types

stockpiling Storing materials in bulk for future use

sued To take someone to a court of law because you believe they have harmed your business or reputation

tourniquets Devices used to stop bleeding by applying pressure

toxic Poisonous or harmful

trade secrets Secret processes used by a company to make products

transplants The insertion or attachment of body parts from another person

U.S. Food & Drug Administration (FDA) A government department that protects the public from unsafe substances

vaccines Preventative medicines that protect people from diseases

virtual reality (VR) A computer simulation that seems realistic

war crimes Crimes committed against an enemy or prisoners of war that go against international agreements, or are unethical and cruel

World Health Organization (WHO) A United Nations organization that works to improve the health of people around the world

LEARNING MORE

BOOKS

Bankston, John. *Frederick Banting and the Discovery of Insulin* (Unlocking the Secrets of Science). Mitchell Lane Publishers, 2001.

Biskup, Agnieszka. *Medical Marvels: The Next 100 Years of Medicine* (Our World: The Next 100 Years). Capstone Press, 2017.

Daniels, Patricia, and Christina Wilsdon. *Ultimate Body-Pedia*. National Geographic Children's Books, 2014.

Jones, Grace. *Medicine and Illness* (Our Values). Crabtree Publishing, 2019.

WEBSITES

http://faculty.washington.edu/chudler/neurok.html
Click "explore" to see the range of neuroscience topics available for you to read.

https://kids.frontiersin.org
Take a look at articles on real scientific discoveries, reviewed by children.

www.mddionline.com/5-coolest-prosthetic-arm-breakthroughs
Discover the coolest artificial limb breakthroughs.

www.ted.com/playlists/23/the_future_of_medicine
Watch this movie to find out how artificial body parts may be printed in future.

INDEX

ABOUT THE AUTHOR

Ellen Rodger is a writer and editor who has written about fleas, hurricanes, potatoes, sewer systems, and solar systems. She enjoys hiking, reading, and hearing people tell their stories.